Get More Local Dental Clients

Joel Erlichson

Table Of Contents

7) Content Marketing for Dental Practices
7.1 Blogging and SEO
7.2 Utilizing Video Content
7.3 Creating Engaging Social Media Content

8) Tracking Success: Metrics and Analytics
8.1 Understanding Google Analytics
8.2 Key Performance Indicators (KPIs) for Dental Practices
8.3 Utilizing A/B Testing for Campaign Improvement

Conclusion: Putting It All Together

Chapter 1: Introduction

Welcome to "Get More Local Dental Clients" - a comprehensive guide designed specifically for dental practices seeking to enhance their client base through the power of strategic marketing. Whether you're just stepping into the world of marketing, or you're looking for innovative ways to connect with potential patients in your local area, this guide is for you.

1.1 Why Local Marketing Matters for Dental Practices

As a dental professional, your primary goal is to provide top-quality dental care - but to achieve this, you first need to attract patients to your practice. This is where local marketing comes into play.

In the realm of dental care, proximity is a key factor. Most patients prefer choosing a dental office within a comfortable travel distance from their home or workplace. Therefore, focusing your marketing efforts on the local community can provide a significant advantage.

Local marketing helps you establish strong relationships with patients in your community, encouraging patient loyalty and word-of-mouth referrals, which are invaluable for any dental practice. Furthermore, local marketing allows you to tailor your marketing efforts to the specific needs, interests, and demographics of your local area, thus making your marketing strategy more effective and efficient.

1.2 The Importance of a Comprehensive Marketing Strategy

While local marketing is essential, it should not stand alone in your quest to attract more patients. Instead, it should be a key component of a broader, comprehensive marketing strategy.

A comprehensive marketing strategy for a dental practice involves a mix of different tactics, both online and offline. This includes a user-friendly, SEO-optimized website, active presence on social media platforms, email marketing, content marketing, direct mail, community engagement, and more.

The aim of a comprehensive marketing strategy is to reach potential patients at multiple touchpoints, increasing the chances of conversion. It also helps to build your brand image, establish credibility, and foster strong relationships with your patients.

In the following chapters, we'll delve deeper into each aspect of a successful marketing strategy for dental practices. We'll offer practical tips, insights, and methods that you can apply to your practice, helping you navigate the world of marketing and attract more local dental clients. Whether you're a marketing novice or just need a refresher, this guide has something to offer you.

2) Understanding Your Target Audience

2.1 Identifying Your Ideal Patient Before you can effectively market your dental practice, you need to understand who your ideal patient is. This goes beyond basic demographics like age and gender. Instead, you should consider factors like:

- **Lifestyle**: Does your ideal patient have a family? What is their occupation?
- **Values**: What do they value when it comes to dental care? For example, are they more concerned with cost, quality, convenience, or a combination of these factors?
- **Dental needs**: Are they looking for general dental care, cosmetic dentistry, pediatric dentistry, orthodontics, etc.?

- **Behavior:** How often do they visit the dentist? What are their habits when it comes to oral health?

Understanding these factors will help you tailor your marketing messages to resonate with your ideal patients, increasing the likelihood that they will choose your practice for their dental care.

2.2 Understanding Local Market Dynamics

The next step is understanding the dynamics of your local market. This involves researching other dental practices in your area to understand what services they offer, their pricing structure, and their marketing strategies.

Consider also the broader socioeconomic factors at play in your area. What is the average income? What is the dominant industry or occupation among residents? What are the primary languages spoken?

This understanding will not only allow you to identify gaps in the market that your practice can fill but also to align your services and marketing efforts with the specific needs and characteristics of your local community.

2.3 Patient's Decision Making Process

Finally, it's crucial to understand your patients' decision-making process. In other words, what factors do they consider when choosing a dentist?

This could be anything from the location of the practice and the services offered, to the personality of the dentist and the atmosphere of the practice.

Surveys or informal conversations can provide valuable insights into what your patients value most in a dental practice. With this information, you can shape your marketing messages to highlight these aspects of your practice, showing potential patients why they should choose you as their dentist.

Remember, the more you understand about your target audience, the more effectively you can reach them with your marketing efforts.

3) Building a Strong Online Presence

3.1 Importance of a Well-Designed, User-Friendly Website

Your website is often the first point of contact between your dental practice and potential patients, making it an integral part of your online presence. An effective website does more than just list your services—it provides valuable information, instills trust, and encourages visitors to book an appointment.

Ensure your website is well-designed and user-friendly, with an intuitive layout, mobile-friendly design, clear calls-to-action, and high-quality images. Include sections on your team, services, patient testimonials, and a blog for dental health tips.

These elements can greatly enhance the user experience and convert visitors into patients.

3.2 Optimizing Your Website for Local SEO

Local Search Engine Optimization (SEO) ensures that your website appears in search results when potential patients in your area search for dental services. This involves keyword optimization, consistent NAP (Name, Address, Phone number) information, and local content creation.

Additionally, ensure your website is technically sound with fast load times, mobile optimization, and secure HTTPS protocol. These factors can significantly impact your local SEO ranking.

3.3 Utilizing Google My Business for Local Visibility

Google My Business (GMB) is a free tool that allows you to manage how your business appears on Google Search and Maps. It's crucial for local businesses, including dental practices, as it increases your visibility on search results and provides potential patients with key information like your location, hours, and reviews.

Ensure your GMB profile is fully completed and regularly updated. Encourage happy patients to leave reviews and respond promptly and professionally to all reviews.

3.4 Importance of Online Reviews and Reputation Management

Online reviews significantly influence a patient's decision when choosing a dentist. Actively seek reviews from satisfied patients and ensure you monitor and respond to all reviews—positive or negative—in a timely and professional manner.

Moreover, address any negative feedback by taking the conversation offline and resolving the issue. This shows potential patients that you value their experience and are committed to high-quality care.

3.5 Leveraging Social Media Platforms

Social media provides a platform to connect with your community, showcase your services, and share valuable dental health content. Regularly post engaging content, interact with your followers, and respond to inquiries promptly.

Consider the platforms your target audience uses most—whether that's Facebook, Instagram, Twitter, or LinkedIn—and establish a consistent presence. Remember, social media is a two-way street; it's not just about promoting your services, but also about engaging with your followers and building relationships.

4) Offline Marketing Techniques

4.1 Direct Mail Campaigns

Despite the surge in digital marketing, direct mail campaigns remain effective, particularly for local businesses. They can be tailored to your target audience and provide a tangible reminder of your dental practice. Consider sending postcards with special offers, newsletters highlighting your services, or reminders for check-ups to households in your local area.

4.2 Community Events and Sponsorships

Participation in community events or sponsoring local teams or events not only increases your visibility but also demonstrates your commitment to the community.

This could be anything from setting up a booth at a local fair, offering free dental check-ups at a community health event, or sponsoring a local sports team. These initiatives can significantly boost your reputation and attract new patients.

4.3 Networking with Other Local Businesses

Building relationships with other local businesses can lead to valuable partnerships and referrals. Consider partnering with local schools, sports teams, or other relevant organizations for mutual promotion. For example, a local health food store might be interested in promoting a dental practice that emphasizes holistic dental care.

4.4 Local Media Advertising

Don't underestimate the power of traditional media. Local newspapers, radio stations, and television channels can still reach a broad audience. Running ads, contributing expert articles, or participating in interviews can boost your visibility and credibility in the community. Ensure your message aligns with your brand and appeals to your target audience.

Remember, while digital marketing is crucial, offline techniques can complement your online efforts, helping to build a comprehensive marketing strategy that effectively reaches your target audience at multiple touchpoints.

5) Digital Advertising for Dentists

5.1 Google Ads for Local Businesses

Google Ads, particularly local search ads, can be a powerful tool for attracting new patients to your dental practice. These ads appear at the top of search results when potential patients in your area search for dental services. To optimize your Google Ads:

- Use location targeting to reach potential patients in your area.
- Incorporate relevant keywords into your ad copy.
- Use ad extensions to provide additional information like your location, phone number, or patient reviews.
- Track your ad performance and adjust your strategy as needed.

5.2 Social Media Advertising

Social media platforms offer sophisticated advertising options that allow you to target your ads to specific demographics, such as people in your area of a certain age or with specific interests.

Facebook and Instagram, for instance, offer a variety of ad formats, including image ads, video ads, carousel ads, and more. They also provide detailed analytics to track the performance of your ads and adjust your strategy as needed.

5.3 Retargeting Ads to Engage Potential Patients

Retargeting, also known as remarketing, is a type of online advertising that allows you to show ads to people who have previously visited your website or interacted with your brand online. This can be a highly effective way to re-engage potential patients who have expressed interest in your services but have not yet booked an appointment.

You can implement retargeting ads through platforms like Google Ads or Facebook Ads. It's a powerful way to keep your dental practice top-of-mind and encourage potential patients to take the next step.

While digital advertising requires an investment, it can be a highly effective way to reach your target audience, increase your online visibility, and attract new patients to your dental practice.

It's all about finding the right mix of strategies that work best for your unique practice and goals.

6) Email Marketing and Patient Retention

6.1 Building an Email List

Building a robust email list is the first step in implementing a successful email marketing strategy. Encourage patients to subscribe to your email list by offering a valuable incentive, such as a free dental care guide or a discount on their first appointment. Remember, obtaining a patient's consent to send them emails is crucial to comply with privacy laws.

6.2 Creating Effective Email Campaigns

Email campaigns can serve various purposes, from welcoming new patients and sharing dental health tips, to promoting your services and special offers. To create effective email campaigns:

Email campaigns can serve various purposes, from welcoming new patients and sharing dental health tips, to promoting your services and special offers. To create effective email campaigns:

- Write compelling subject lines to encourage recipients to open your emails.

- Provide valuable content to keep your patients engaged.

- Include clear calls-to-action to guide patients on what to do next.
- Segment your email list to send targeted messages to specific groups of patients.
- Monitor your email metrics to understand what works and what doesn't.

6.3 Using Email for Appointment Reminders and Patient Retention

Email is an effective tool for sending appointment reminders, thereby reducing no-shows and encouraging regular check-ups. You can also use email to follow up with patients after their appointment, perhaps asking for feedback or providing post-care instructions.

Furthermore, regular email communication can enhance patient retention by keeping your practice top-of-mind and demonstrating your ongoing commitment to your patients' dental health.

Remember, while email marketing can be highly effective, it's important to respect your patients' inboxes and only send emails that provide real value.

7) Content Marketing for Dental Practices

7.1 Blogging and SEO

Blogging is a powerful tool for demonstrating your expertise, providing value to your patients, and improving your website's SEO. Regularly post articles on your blog covering topics that your patients care about, such as dental health tips, explanations of dental procedures, or answers to common dental health questions.

Ensure your blog posts are optimized for SEO, including relevant keywords, internal and external links, and meta descriptions. This can improve your website's visibility on search engine results, making it easier for potential patients to find your practice.

7.2 Utilizing Video Content

Video content is increasingly popular and can be a highly engaging way to showcase your dental practice. Consider creating videos introducing your team, providing a tour of your office, explaining dental procedures, or offering oral health advice.

Videos can be posted on your website, shared on social media, or uploaded to YouTube. Just ensure your videos are professional, informative, and short enough to keep viewers' attention.

7.3 Creating Engaging Social Media Content

Social media is ideal for sharing bite-sized, engaging content.

Post a mix of content types, such as dental health tips, patient testimonials, behind-the-scenes glimpses of your practice, and team highlights.

Engage with your followers by responding to comments and messages promptly. You could also host Q&A sessions, polls, or contests to increase engagement.

Remember, content marketing isn't just about promoting your services—it's about providing value to your audience. The more valuable your content, the more likely potential patients are to trust your practice and choose you for their dental care needs.

8) Tracking Success: Metrics and Analytics

8.1 Understanding Google Analytics

Google Analytics is a powerful tool for understanding how people find and interact with your website. You can track metrics like the number of visitors, how long they stay on your site, which pages they visit, and whether they take actions like booking an appointment or subscribing to your newsletter.

Take the time to understand how to use Google Analytics and regularly review your data. This can provide valuable insights into what's working in your marketing strategy and what areas need improvement.

8.2 Key Performance Indicators (KPIs) for Dental Practices

Key Performance Indicators (KPIs) are measurable values that demonstrate how effectively your dental practice is achieving key business objectives. Some important KPIs for dental practices might include:

- New patient acquisition: How many new patients are you attracting?
- Patient retention rate: What percentage of patients return to your practice?
- Appointment no-show rate: How often do patients miss their appointments?
- Revenue growth: Is your practice's revenue increasing?
- Patient satisfaction: How satisfied are your patients with their experience at your practice?

By tracking these KPIs, you can assess the effectiveness of your marketing efforts and make data-driven decisions to improve your strategy.

8.3 Utilizing A/B Testing for Campaign Improvement

A/B testing, also known as split testing, involves comparing two versions of a marketing campaign to see which performs better. For example, you might test two different email subject lines, two different landing page designs, or two different ad copies.

By analyzing the results of your A/B tests, you can gain insights into what resonates with your audience and use these insights to improve your future campaigns.

Remember, the goal of tracking metrics and analytics is not just to gather data, but to use that data to make informed decisions that drive your dental practice's growth and success.

Conclusion: Putting It All Together

As we've explored in this guide, attracting more local dental clients involves a combination of effective online and offline marketing strategies. From understanding your target audience to building a strong online presence, leveraging digital advertising, utilizing email marketing, creating valuable content, and tracking your success, each step plays a crucial role in your overall marketing strategy.

But remember, there's no one-size-fits-all approach to dental marketing. What works for one practice may not work for another. It's important to understand your unique practice, your community, and your patients, and tailor your marketing efforts accordingly.

Start by implementing one or two strategies, track your results, and adjust your approach based on what works best for your practice. Over time, you'll find the right mix of marketing tactics that allow you to attract and retain more patients, grow your practice, and establish yourself as a trusted dental provider in your community.

Remember, marketing is not a one-and-done task—it's an ongoing process of learning, adapting, and improving. But with patience, persistence, and a patient-centric approach, you can successfully attract more local dental clients and achieve your practice's goals.

Thank you for reading this guide. Here's to your success in attracting more local dental clients!

Thank You